ski·ing

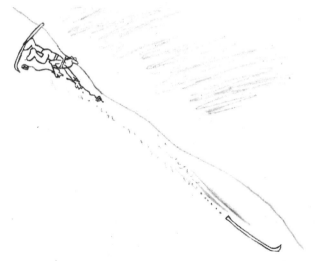

ski·ing

a snowslider's dictionary

by Henry Beard
and Roy McKie

Workman Publishing · New York

Copyright © 2002 by Henry Beard and Roy McKie

All rights reserved. No portion of this book may be reproduced—mechanically, electronically, or by any other means, including photocopying—without written permission of the publisher. Published simultaneously in Canada by Thomas Allen & Son Limited.

Library of Congress Cataloging-in-Publication Data

Beard, Henry
    Ski.ing : a snowslider's dictionary / by Henry Beard and Roy McKie.
      p. cm.
    ISBN 978-0-7611-2820-5 (alk. paper)
    1. Skis and skiing—Humor. I. McKie, Roy. II. Title.

PN6231.S549 B43 2002
796.93'02'07—dc21
                                                 2002025894

Workman books are available at special discounts when purchased in bulk for premiums and sales promotions as well as for fund-raising or educational use. Special editions can also be created to specification. For details, contact the Special Sales Director at the address below.

Workman Publishing Company, Inc.
225 Varick Street
New York, NY 10014-4381
www.workman.com

Printed in the United States of America

First printing: August 2002

10   9   8   7   6   5   4   3

To all those who have heard the call of the slopes.

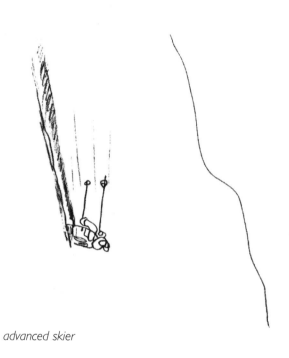

advanced skier

advanced skier

Anyone who can remain standing while skiing down a mountain for as long as he or she stood in line waiting to go up. See BEGINNER, INTERMEDIATE SKIER, and EXPERT.

aerials
Competitive ski jumping in which daredevils perform midair acrobatics, with points awarded for length of hospital stay, size of bill, originality of X rays, complexity of surgery, and creativity in filling out disability claims as measured by speed and amount of payment.

aerials

all-mountain

Common descriptive term for boots or skis that are designed to perform equally poorly under a wide variety of conditions and over many different types of terrain.

Alpine Formal name for downhill skiing, one of a half-dozen distinct styles found in the sport. The others are Nordic (cross-country), Norpine (telemarking), Fanatic (powder skiing), Moronic (tree-skiing in wooded glades), Asinine (snowboarding), and Supine (reclining on a sofa in a nice cozy lodge with a feigned ski injury).

altitude sickness

Term for a variety of maladies
brought on by breathing the
oxygen-deprived atmosphere
at a mountain ski resort that
include the common symptoms
of headache, dizziness, vertigo,
nausea, and insomnia, as well as
a number of less well-known
conditions like Shackleton's

Disease (a love of being cold), the Icarus Complex (an indifference to heights), Tussaud's Complaint (a compulsion to apply wax to things), the Bozo Syndrome (an impulse to wear garish articles of clothing), and Rocky Mountain Ski Shop Fever (an overpowering urge to dispose of excess cash).

American teaching method

Simplified, accelerated system of ski instruction in which students are taught how to operate a hot tub before they learn how to execute the snowplow.

ankle Flexible foot joint that, when properly stiffened, permits a skier to transfer the incredible energy stored in a tense jaw, stiff neck, taut shoulders, tight back, rigid hips, and locked knees directly to the base of a pair of rapidly skidding skis.

anticipation

The first of the six basic phases of the classic ski turn, followed in rapid succession by Initiation, Trepidation, Desperation, Exclamation, and Recuperation. See PREJUMP and TURN.

antifriction device

Teflon pad designed to promote smooth binding release, one of the most recent of a whole host of injury-preventing features, large and small, that have, amazingly enough, made skiing down a mountain actually safer than staying home and falling off the roof of your own house.

après-ski Term for ski resort activities following a long day on the slopes, which typically include le bitch and le moan, le soaking of les tootsies, la long nap, le stiff drink, le big wait at la fancy dump for le lousy meal, and le checking on le airline to see if they have la earlier flight home.

après-ski

artificial snow

Layer of man-made frozen ice crystals
created by spraying a fine jet of water
out of high-pressure nozzles into very
cold air that is identical to a real snowfall
in all but one respect: even the lightest
sleeper will not sit bolt upright in bed
at 5:00 A.M. if a couple of inches of
natural snow begin to fall.

avalanche

The only thing likely to come down a mountain that is more dangerous than a slope full of skiers. See "TRACK LEFT" & "TRACK RIGHT."

balancing

The process in which
a skier continuously shifts
his or her weight from the
wrong side of the right
ski to the right side of
the wrong ski. See EDGES
and INSIDE & OUTSIDE SKI.

bare spot A place
where, due to insufficient
snowfall, the underlying earth is
visible. Depending on weather
conditions, bare spots can range
from a patch the size of a
footprint to a patch the size of
the northeastern United States.

base *1.* The layer of snow on the surface of a ski slope. *2.* The layer of plastic on the base of a ski that is no longer there because *1* is no longer there.

bastard

1. Wide, flat, single-cut file used to flatten, sharpen, or bevel ski edges. 2. Someone who charged you for hand-filing your skis but used a belt sander instead.

bathroom

bathroom Sanitary facility with a "closed for cleaning" sign on its door located at the bottom of a long flight of stairs just past the handy benches where you put on your ski boots.

bed-and-breakfast

Quiet, informal, family-style ski-area lodging whose one major advantage over a hotel is that you are not going to run into someone in a bar, elevator, or lobby that you ran into earlier in the day coming down the ski slope.

bed-and-breakfast

beginner Newcomer to the slopes who has to rely on simple ignorance to bring about skiing mishaps that he or she will eventually learn to cause through sheer stupidity.

belt bag
Small zippered fanny pack worn at the waist just above the rump that is a superb shock absorber for bruising backward falls since it is usually filled with a dense, body-cushioning substance made of crushed candy bars, a wad of old lift tickets stuck together with sunscreen, and a burst packet of hand-warmer fluid.

bigfoot

bigfoot Giant, hairy, reclusive humanoid said to inhabit remote mountain areas which probably does not exist, but if it does and it ever decides to take up skiing, it's in luck because resort rental shops have a remarkably large selection of boots that appear to have been designed exclusively for its use.

binding
Ingenious automatic mechanism mounted on a ski that can hold it clamped tightly to a boot when subjected to a force that would deform a bridge abutment and yet still permit it to drop off the foot of a skier who sneezes while riding a chairlift.

binding

bluebird

bluebird Slang term for

a day of absolutely ideal skiing weather, with blue skies and perfect powder snow, usually followed by a week or two of days with less satisfactory conditions known as turkey, grouse, mudhen, nutcracker, brown thrasher, albatross, buzzard, mockingbird, and bird doo.

bones

The fact that there are 206 bones in the adult human body may alarm novice skiers, but it's worth noting that according to medical records two of them, the stapes of the left and right inner ear, have never been broken in any reported skiing accident.

boogy Slang term for skiing flat
out, one of several bits of beach jargon
that surfers brought to the slopes, a favor
skiing has not returned, probably because
of the low appeal of the "schusser" look
(runny nose, chapped lips, and a limb in
a cast) and the Germanic roots of the
sport, which provide poor substitutes
for snappy words like "bummer"
(*zum kotzen*), "far out" (*träumerisch*),
"hot dog" (*Bockwurst*), "dude" (*Mann*),
and "wipeout" (*Ausradierung*).

boot A pain in the ass that fits on the foot. See CONVENIENCE BOOT, CONVENTIONAL BOOT, DOUBLE BOOT, ORTHOTIC, OUTER SHELL, SOCK, and THOR.

boot bag

A sack designed to be carried over the shoulder with a large central compartment that holds a pair of ski boots and enough zippered side pockets to contain all the pills, tablets, capsules, lotions, ointments, creams, salves, gauze pads, and bandages you will need to take, apply, or affix after wearing a pair of ski boots for a day.

bowl Wide-open, steep, rocky areas above the tree line where even simple plants with the limited intellects found among members of the vegetable kingdom have enough sense not to go.

buckle Highly adjustable snap-shut closure device that permits a skier to easily and quickly change the fit of a boot from a little too tight to just a bit too loose.

bump

1. A swelling resulting from *2,* a blow caused by tripping over *3,* an elevated mound of snow. See MOGUL and MOGUL SKIING.

bunny slope

Condescending term for a gentle hill where beginners ski, as opposed to more hazardous and challenging advanced and expert trails, which are known as guinea pig slopes, lemming slopes, and jackass slopes.

camber

A built-in convexity found in most skis, varying in depth of curve among different models and manufacturers. Other areas of variation in ski design include "sidecut," the degree of taper in the waist; "splay," the steepness of curve of the tip; "flex," the amount of torsional movement in the body of the ski; "float," the ability of the ski to maneuver in deep powder; "damping," the capacity of the ski to absorb vibration; "swingweight," the weight distribution over the ski's length; "repellence," the ugliness of coloration, trademarks, and designs on the topskin of the ski; "flingstrength," the ski's resistance to mishandling by airline personnel; "scathe," the rate of deterioration of the ski when dumped in a hall closet for the summer; "swipe-risk," the ski's attractiveness to a potential thief; "slopelife," the period of time before it becomes hopelessly obsolete; and "searchlength," the amount of time its owner would spend looking for it if it flew off a ski rack into deep snow by the side of a road at four o'clock on a Sunday afternoon.

camber

carrying skis

carrying skis

Even when held tightly together by straps or interlocking ski brakes, a pair of skis can be awkward to manage. To master the knack of carrying them, have a friend stand close behind you on your right or left side. Place the skis over your shoulder, with the tips forward and the bindings just touching your back, and drape your arm over their top surfaces. Now pivot on your hips slowly in both directions as if looking at the scenery or an attractive individual of the opposite sex. The last foot or so of your skis should hit your friend at about ear level. If you're grazing the top of your friend's head or shoulders, adjust your grip, increase the speed of your hip turn, or flatten the slope of the ski-carrying angle.

carrying skis

carving

The art of making precise, skidless turns with the sharp edge of a ski, so called because the maneuver leaves deeply carved grooves in the snow when performed by an expert and ice carvings, rock carvings, and tree carvings when attempted by a novice.

catching air

Slang term for a jump performed on skis, which is usually followed by catching hell from the skier you hit or catching a ride to the hospital. See JUMP and TERRAIN PARK.

catching an edge

Accidentally letting the edge of a ski dig into the snow, one of the 100 most common causes of falling during a ski run. See EDGES and FALL.

catwalk
A narrow connecting trail cut laterally across a slope or along a ridge with a steep drop-off on one side, so called because it is normally just wide enough to permit two very careful, surefooted, medium-size, shorthaired cats to pass one another safely.

chairlift Transportation system found at ski resorts in which a series of chairs suspended from a cable rapidly conveys anywhere from one to six skiers at a time from the front of one line to the back of another.

chairlift

chalet

chalet Word that traditionally appears in the name of any motel located within 50 miles of a ski mountain. See DUMP.

citizen race A cross-country marathon open to amateur Nordic skiers. The most famous are the historic 53-mile Vasaloppet in Sweden and the traditional 22-mile Birkebeiner in Wisconsin, but a pair of less well-known yet equally demanding modern races are growing in popularity: Vermont's grueling

Saabslog, in which teams of burly skiers attempt to tow a disabled vehicle from a ski resort parking lot to a gas station 14 miles away, and Colorado's brutal Baggageblunder, in which skiers on ill-fitting rental equipment traverse a special 18-mile circuit around the Denver airport searching for their lost luggage.

clinic Special course of study undertaken by a skier in an effort to correct the one fundamental flaw that has allowed him or her to successfully compensate for a huge number of minor mistakes. See LESSON.

code

1. A set of rules governing how a skier should behave on the slopes. *2.* A stuffed-up node that a skier cad get from staddig aroud id wet clode id a lift lide.

comma Curved posture
used for standing on or traversing
a ski slope, with the hips and
knees thrust inward toward
the hill and the head and torso
angled outward, as opposed
to the more common skiing
postures known as the question
mark, the exclamation point, the
hyphen, the asterisk, and the dash.

condominium

Apartment in a winter resort area purchased by avid skiers who like the idea of having direct access to the slopes from a conveniently located mountain of debt. See SKI IN, SKI OUT.

convenience boot

Term for a rear-entry Alpine ski boot with an internal cable system that makes it possible for a skier to produce total discomfort over the entire foot with a single motion of a preset lever.

conventional boot

Term for a front-entry Alpine ski boot with a number of micro-adjustable buckles and dozens of cuff-angle, forward-lean, and flexibility settings that make it possible for a skier to produce a welt, bruise, blister, or pinch at any desired point on the foot.

corduroy Slang term for the neatly raked look of freshly groomed snow, as opposed to the variety of less appealing surface conditions encountered by most skiers, like dropcloth, pool tarp, pup tent, adobe, cobblestone, bric-a-brac, stucco, particleboard, and bubblewrap.

cross-country skiing

Recreational pole-powered backwoods ski touring on Nordic equipment, usually along trails in scenic wilderness areas. More and more skiers have discovered the pleasures of gliding through the peaceful, snow-hushed woods, far from the noise and crowds of the ski slopes, moving with the restful rhythm of the classic free-heel step, with the fresh tang of pine sap wafting on the breezes and no sound but the whispery hiss of the skis slipping through the snow, the soft slapping of the loose backpack flap, the muffled tinkle of the car keys dropping into the puffy powder of a deep, wind-sculpted drift, the inaudible beep as the cold-depleted cell phone battery goes completely dead, the sharp, crisp snap of a ski binding breaking, and the eerie wail of elemental rage as man comes to grips with the ancient forces of nature.

cross-country skiing

curved ski poles

1. Expert skier's poles bent at the factory to fit around the body and thus improve control and reduce air resistance. *2.* Beginner's poles bent during use to fit around trees, trail signs, and chairlift pylons.

day area Ski facility without overnight accommodations where, after spending several hours dodging the dolts on the slopes, you get to spend several hours dodging the same dolts on the roads.

demo skis

Abbreviated term for skis loaned to prospective purchasers for on-slope tryouts (*demonstration skis*) and for the same skis following their conversion into rental equipment after about a month of such trials (*demolition skis*).

destination resort
Full-service ski facility that offers not just lift lines, but also locker lines, front desk lines, elevator lines, shuttle bus lines, restaurant lines, and movie lines.

DIN

Abbreviation for *Deutsche Industrie Norm*, or German Industrial Standard, a set of internationally accepted measurements that includes the settings for ski bindings. A chart produced by German engineers provides ski shops with precise instructions for setting the release point for toe and heel bindings based on the weight, physical structure, and bone strength of individual skiers, their grooming and personal hygiene, their posture while standing at strict attention, their knowledge of the applicable rules and regulations, their overall cooperativeness with the proper authorities, and their readiness at all times to do exactly as they are told without sniveling like the miserable, inferior weaklings they are.

double black diamond

Trail-marking symbol indicating a very difficult run for experts only, with a slope greater than 40% or 22°, that is generally attempted only by someone with skis no less than 180 cm long and an IQ no higher than 90. See TRAIL RATING.

double boot

Modern two-piece ski boot designed so that the part that won't close correctly is separate from the part that doesn't fit properly. See INNER BOOT and OUTER SHELL.

double-pole push

Method of crossing flat terrain by propelling oneself forward with simultaneous pole pushes, a strenuous motion that helps to develop the muscles skiers need at the end of a trip to cram 150 pounds of lumpy ski equipment into a couple of suitcases and still have enough upper-arm strength to pound their fists in rage on the counter at the hotel, the rental car office, and the airline.

downhill
The ultimate form of top-level competition skiing in which racers achieve speeds high enough to complete a challenging, mountain-length course filled with tricky turns and treacherous jumps in the few brief seconds between television commercials.

dryland training

dryland training

A physical workout or practice session undertaken off the slopes or out of skiing season. There are a number of exercises and drills that can help skiers develop the stamina and techniques they need for the sport. Here are a few of the best:

- Stand in one place for five minutes, then take 2 steps forward. Repeat.

- Attach a cinder block to each foot with old belts or duct tape and walk up and down a flight of stairs.

- Sit on a window ledge with your skis in your lap for 30 minutes.

- Tie your ankles together, lie flat on the floor, then, holding a banana in each hand, get to your feet.

- Put a car in neutral and push it for 100 yards.

- Grasp a credit card in your nonwriting hand, then sign your name 100 times.

dryland training

dump

dump *1.* Sudden, heavy snowfall. 2. Low-rent ski-area lodging that still looks like a hovel even after being covered by a scenic layer of soft, white powder after a sudden, heavy snowfall.

edges One of two sharpened metal strips on the sides of a ski, either the edge your weight should be on or the edge your weight is actually on.

edging
1. Key skill in which a skier uses a rolling motion of the knees and hips to tilt the ski edges into the slope in order to stand still on the fall line. *2.* Key skill in which a skier uses a series of hip movements and shoulder turns to gain several places in the lift line.

egg Descriptive term for a crouched or tucked body position used by skiers to eliminate air resistance on a fast, straight downhill run, often followed by the Dropped Egg, the Egg Roll, the Scrambled Egg, and the Omelet.

egg

elasticity

Measure of a binding's ability to yield slightly before releasing, expressed as RCT (Return to Center Time). Other gauges of a binding's qualities are its TBSGS (Time Before Something Goes Sproing), COR (Cost Of Repair), and DBIBITSA (Days Before It's Back In The Shop Again).

expert Savvy, seasoned, trail-smart skier who has sufficiently mastered the complex art of navigating the slopes to be able to repeatedly execute downhill runs at a mountain without ever skidding, falling, or paying.

extreme skiing

1. Acrobatic skiing performed on slopes or jumps by professionals, with moves like the Outrigger, the Backscratcher, the Möbius Flip, the Space Walk, and the Wongbanger. *2.* Idiosyncratic slipping and sliding done by amateurs on icy flats and bare spots with moves like the Gogglescratcher, the Face Plant, the Pole Trip, and the Yard Sale.

fall

Out of simple politeness, the word "fall" should never be used in skiing. For the noun, substitute "parka carve," "whole-body edging," or "stem-to-stern turn"; for the verb, use "pronify" or "recumbulate"; and replace the adjective "fallen" with "unup," "deverticalized," or "formerly perpendicular."

92 | A SNOWSLIDER'S DICTIONARY

fall line Imaginary line
following the steepest and most
direct path down a slope that
skiers continuously traverse on
a run, often stopping at other
invisible slope features along the
way like the Topple Corridor, the
Tumble Lane, the Stagger Path,
and the Stumble Zone.

fat Adjective that provides a reliable way of dividing snowboarders by age into two distinct groups: those who use it as a synonym of "excellent" and those who use it as a synonym of "corpulent."

fear A perfectly normal human feeling of anxiety experienced at the start of a ski run that you can easily overcome once you realize that if you drove for hours on an icy, winding road full of homicidal morons, or flew halfway across the country on an airline whose ordinary operations routinely violate all of the protocols of the Geneva Convention, and then rode to the top of a steep mountain on a complicated cable-driven mechanism operated by a ski resort company that is incapable of brewing a cup of coffee, chances are, as a practical matter, the worst is probably behind you.

filled garment

Puffy outerwear usually packed with down harvested from geese in a humane procedure in which tame flocks of the hefty fowl are shown pictures of just how dorky people look in jackets stuffed with their feathers and the stunned birds molt on the spot.

filled garment

flat light
Low-angle, late-afternoon midwinter sunlight that provides poor visibility of skiing terrain, so named because its interesting effects are best appreciated and most often observed from a position flat on the ground.

geländesprung

German term for a daring aerial maneuver in which a skier uses a powerful pole push to jump from the edge of a bump, ridge, or slope in order to clear an obstacle by leaping completely over it, pronounced "godDAMNwhataSTUPIDthingtodo."

gloves

Hand coverings that are too warm on hot days and too cold on chilly ones, tight enough to restrict circulation but too bulky for manual dexterity, capable of admitting moisture from the outside without letting dampness escape from within, and too large to fit into a pocket but still light enough to disappear from sight several minutes before their absence is noted.

goggles

Eye-protecting lenses that greatly reduce the sun's potentially damaging glare by using a tiny amount of trapped moisture to produce, directly in front of the wearer's eyes, a dense layer of light-absorbing fog.

gondola
Ski lift consisting of a series of small enclosed cabins suspended from a continuously moving overhead cable to which they are attached by an operator when fully loaded. It's a fast and easy way to ascend a mountain unless you suffer from acrophobia (fear of heights), claustrophobia (fear of confined

spaces), fatsophobia (fear of being sat on by an obese individual), nokiaphobia (fear of having to listen to loud cell phone conversations), velcrophobia (fear of becoming fastened to someone else's pocket flap), or autoparkasphyxiaphobia (fear of being smothered by your own down-filled ski jacket).

gravity

One of the five fundamental forces that affect skiers. The others are the strong force, which jams their bindings; the weak force, which causes their ankles to wobble; electromagnetism, which makes their car batteries go dead; and the cosmological constant, which produces continuous expansion in their waistlines. See INERTIA.

gravity

grooming report

grooming report

Daily account of the state of the current snow cover at a ski area, usually described by a few common terms like packed powder (wet slush), packed powder (glare ice), packed powder (frozen granules), packed powder (broken crust), and packed powder (bare earth). See LIFT STATUS.

hat Headgear that provides the skier with protection against the cold in exact inverse proportion to its ability to provide immunity from ridicule.

headband

1. Insulated elasticized cloth strip designed to keep the ears warm while making it easy to wear headphones while skiing so that, as you fly down the slopes, you can listen to 2. The Grateful Dead.

heli-skiing Off-trail

skiing in which skiers are flown to remote, empty, untouched slopes where they can experience the thrill of pure powder skiing as well as the challenge of heli-praying-the-stupid-thing-doesn't-crash, heli-finding-somewhere-to-go-to-the-bathroom, and heli-figuring-out-how-to-pay-the-stupendous-bill.

helmet
Hard-shelled, impact-proof headgear designed to prevent brain injuries that is rarely worn by skiers since any individual who thinks it's fun to descend a steep slope at high speed in subzero weather obviously lacks a vital organ above the neck that requires any special protection.

herringbone

Method of climbing a slope using short duckwalking steps with the tails of the skis together and the tips apart which, though tiring and time-consuming, has the advantage that you never have to look down the hill, no one wants to race you, it's a snap to come to a full stop, and you have an hour from the time you first see a tree until you hit it.

herringbone

high-speed lift

Very fast, detachable chairlift that can deposit a skier on the top of the mountain while his or her skis and poles are still waiting in the lift line below.

hot tub

Circular therapeutic bathing pool where, after a long day on the slopes, skiers can get into hot water with their loved ones, or get into hot water with their loved ones.

hypothermia

Potentially life-threatening condition caused by lowered body temperature that needlessly worries skiers who really should be more concerned about thermowieniea (hotdogging), hypercerveza (excessive beer consumption), albertotombamania (delusion of skill), and omniposteriosis (behaving like a total buttwipe).

ice Frozen surface hated by skiers who don't take the time to pause and marvel at the fact that the same hardworking, versatile compound that in its other states can drown you in a resort swimming pool or scald you in a sauna can also trip you up and knock you senseless on a ski slope.

inertia

The tendency of a skier's body to resist changes in direction or speed due to the action of Newton's First Law of Motion. Other physical laws that affect skiers include:

- Two objects of greatly different mass falling side by side will have the same rate of descent, but the lighter one is going to have much larger hospital bills.

- Matter can be neither created nor destroyed, but if it drops out of a parka pocket while you're riding the chairlift, don't expect to encounter it again in this universe.

- No two bodies can occupy precisely the same location at exactly the same time unless the gondola loader is a true professional.

- Every action taught by one ski instructor is opposed by an equally qualified ski instructor with an opposite point of view.

- When an irresistible force meets an immovable object, an unethical lawyer will immediately appear.

- What goes up, must wait.

- A body at rest will remain at rest even after it is acted upon by an outside force unless that force also opens the blinds, turns the radio on loud, and takes away the covers.

inertia

injury

injury

Impairment caused by a skiing accident that past studies seemed to show was more likely to occur on the last run of the day, when skiers are tired, but new evidence suggests the opposite: that skiers are more vulnerable when they are overeager and impulsive, and if they simply eliminate that alluring but potentially disastrous *first* run of the day, their odds of injury are reduced to zero.

inner boot

Soft, pliable interior part of an Alpine ski boot which, if it didn't pinch, would keep the foot, if the right socks had been worn, firmly and comfortably in place if the outer shell didn't bind. See OUTER SHELL and SOCK.

inside & outside ski

Terms used by instructors to describe, respectively, the uphill and downhill ski at the beginning of a turn, which, depending on the direction of the fall, become either the inside-out or upside-down ski at its completion.

intermediate skier

Someone who has successfully progressed to the point that most of the time when he or she falls, it's due to a collision with another skier. See RECREATIONAL SKIER.

instructor

Canny individual who, after years of struggling to profit from his or her own skiing mistakes, has finally figured out how to profit from other people's. See PROFESSIONAL SKIER.

J-bar

A drag lift that can trip, snag, sideswipe, wrench, flip, bonk, bash, or clobber only one skier at a time. See T-BAR.

jet turn *1.* A turn that is initiated by propelling the feet forward and unweighting the skis. *2.* A turn that is canceled because of equipment problems, or is made with an unplanned stop, or is diverted to an unintended destination.

jump

Aerial maneuver undertaken from a man-made or naturally occurring terrain feature by someone who, because he has the brain of a bird, believes he can fly like one.

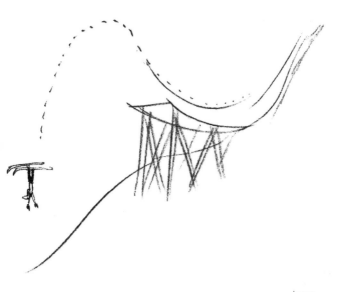

jump

kick turn Technique
for skiing a winding trail using
one or more 180° turns made
by lifting and pivoting the skis.
A less demanding method of
tackling very curvy terrain is
simply to change direction and
head to a different, less trying
trail with a maneuver known
as a punt turn.

klister

A thick ski wax that komes out of the tube in a klumsy klotted klump of klinging krud. See TWO-WAX SYSTEM and WAXLESS SKIS.

knapsack A bag used by skiers to carry around a large knumber of things that knobody ever ends up kneeding.

knee
Other than the ego and the wallet, the most sensitive and vulnerable part of a skier. See ORTHOTIC and SHIN.

layering

Wearing several thin articles of clothing rather than a single thick one, which not only provides superior insulation and better wind protection, but also increases the odds that in the faddy, fast-changing world of ski styles, something you're wearing on some part of your body will be in fashion for some portion of your ski trip.

lesson Formal period of instruction during which skiers discover that what they thought they were doing wrong is the only thing they're doing right. See TEACHING SYSTEM and VIDEOTAPE.

lift line

1. A group of people waiting to board a ski lift. 2. A remark or observation used to initiate a conversation with an attractive individual in a lift line, such as "You know, I could spot it a mile away—you're an outdoorsy sort of person, aren't you?" or "What a coincidence! We're both wearing the same number of skis!"

lift line

lift pass
Small card that provides unlimited use of a ski area's facilities for a fixed period of time ranging from a day to a whole skiing season, although a few resorts with rough terrain and a poor safety record also offer unlimited lifetime passes for about half the price of a season ticket.

lift status Portion of
a resort's daily grooming report
that indicates whether the lift
you were planning to use is
temporarily out of service,
not operating due to weather
conditions, shut down for
regular maintenance, closed
for the day, or closed for the
rest of the season.

loading Term for getting on a ski lift, a complicated process that is an entertaining blend of hopscotch, leapfrog, musical chairs, and Russian roulette. See QUAD LIFT.

lodge Large public building at the base of a mountain where skiers taking a break from the lift lines stand in line for the cafeteria and the bathroom.

long johns

Familiar term for full-body underwear, also sometimes referred to as Short Johns, Weird Johns, Bad Johns, Incredible Shrinking Johns, and The Thing That Came From The Laundromat.

maze Path by a line
indirect followed that
often and confusing to
a chairlift leads, a corral
referred to sometimes as.

microclimates

Weather conditions vary dramatically in skiing. For example, on a day when it's 15° and windy on top of the mountain, it may be late fall around your waist, a tropical afternoon in your gloves, an early spring day with heavy showers under your turtleneck, and midnight on Pluto at your toes.

microclimates

millimeter

Along with the centimeter and the meter, common metric measures encountered in ski equipment and competitions, although the traditional English system remains in use at U.S. ski resorts where the height of mountains is still indicated in feet, near misses are measured in inches, and the distance to the nearest bathroom is almost always given in miles.

mitten A large padded shoe worn on the hand. See ZIPPER.

mogul
A bump or mound of snow formed by turns made by skiers in soft snow. The word was once thought to be derived from *mugel,* an Alpine term for a hump or knoll, but more likely candidates are *meugul,* a nasty surprise; *mögulungen,* to turn upside down; *gehmögell,* to curse; or *moogal,* a large bruise.

mogul

mogul skiing

1. Competitive event in which aggressive professional skiers are judged on their speed, style, and control as they race down steep, heavily contoured slopes. 2. Competitive event in which aggressive amateur skiers are judged on the length of their cigars, the size of their portfolios, the compactness of their cell phones, the square footage of their mountainside vacation homes, the contents of their wine cellars, the elaborateness of their home entertainment centers, the tonnage of their sports utility vehicles, and the attractiveness of their trophy wives.

mountain

The word used to describe an unusually large mogul at ski areas in the midwestern United States and the Canadian prairie provinces.

never-ever

Informal term for a complete newcomer to skiing who, one way or the other, is about to fall for the sport and ski for hours on end.

night skiing

Form of skiing done after dark on specially illuminated slopes that makes it possible for skiers to be skiing at the same time they're having a skiing nightmare.

Nordic ski

Long, narrow, lightweight ski designed to alternately grip and glide over the snow surface when its base is coated with waxes other than the ones you happen to have on hand.

Nordic ski binding

Metal clamping device of various designs and widths affixed to cross-country skis which will hold firmly in place the toe tabs of a pair of boots other than the ones you're wearing.

Nordic ski boot

Lightweight lace-up boot designed to attach to a Nordic ski binding at the front but remain free at the rear to provide enough movement to permit a blister to form on the heel while still producing sufficient constriction to allow a bruise to develop just over the middle joint of the big toe.

nursery slope

nursery slope

A gentle hill reserved for beginning skiers, so named because in such areas there is a great deal of whining and crying, most of the motion is done on all fours, no one can figure out how to go to the bathroom, and everyone wants to go home.

off-piste *1.* Descriptive term for ungroomed areas of a mountain that lack defined trails. 2. Descriptive term for a skier who is both irate and dyslexic.

orthotic Custom-made ski boot arch support that can be obtained from any reliable podiatrist, chiropodist, extortionist, or sadist.

outer shell

Hard, plastic exterior part of
an Alpine ski boot which, if it
weren't a size too large, would
hold the lower leg tightly in place
if the inner boot hadn't worn
thin and couldn't be replaced
because it was discontinued by
the manufacturer.

package rate

Plan offered by ski resorts in which the price for lodging also includes, at no extra charge, transport to the rooms by high-speed elevator or reliable, easy-to-use stairs; all-day key storage "on the house"; and complimentary lessons in the lobby on basic ski skills like standing in line and paying for things.

packing out

Technical term used by ski boot salesmen for the process of normal wear during which a boot liner that starts out being a little too tight gradually, over time, remains a little too tight.

parka Outer garment that provides skiers with their chief opportunity to make a fashion statement, although for some reason most skiers prefer to make a fashion speech, a fashion tirade, a fashion diatribe, a fashion indictment, a fashion threat, a fashion ultimatum, or a fashion declaration of war.

pole

pole One of a pair of pointed metal sticks carried by skiers to ensure that they will have something hard and sharp to land on even if they fall on a perfectly groomed ski slope.

pole plant

Term for the motion a skier makes in placing the ski pole into the snow to facilitate a turn. Instructors prefer "pole touch" to emphasize the delicacy of the movement, but most skiers use a simpler and more effective maneuver known as a pole jab, pole lunge, pole wallop, pole pummel, pole driver, or pole dozer.

pole strap

Leather or fabric loop attached to the grip of a ski pole. Whether you loop the straps around your wrists or not depends on whether in a fall you're willing to risk losing your poles or prefer to risk knowing precisely where your poles are without even seeing them.

polyethylene

Synthetic substance used in the manufacture of ski bases which, along with the polyurethane employed in ski boots and the polypropylene found in ski garments, has revolutionized the sport in the last few decades. Among the new space-age materials that promise similar advances in years to come are polyindigestylene, a styrene sandwich filling now being tested at mountaintop lunch spots; polynothine, a polymer resin that will soon replace the few remaining natural fibers in hotel towels; and polyexorbitane, a thermoplastic that will make it possible for every item sold in ski village shops to be molded from the same costly yet amazingly cheesy-looking substance.

pomalift
Ski lift consisting of a series of steel rods with disks on the end that skiers straddle to ride uphill, named after its inventor, Jean Pomagalski, who stumbled on its design by accident while trying to make an automatic spanking machine for the French school system.

powder A deep layer of nice, fresh, light, fluffy snow that falls a week before you arrive at a ski resort or the day after you leave. See SPRING SKIING.

prejump Maneuver in which an expert skier makes a controlled jump just before reaching a bump, mogul, or slope crest. Beginners in a similar situation can execute a controlled prefall just prior to losing their balance and precede it with a prescream, a precurse, and a few pregroans.

1

2

3

4

prejump

professional skier

Individual who believes that if you're going to spend a significant amount of time risking your neck and freezing your butt off, you really ought to get paid for it. See RECREATIONAL SKIER.

quad lift

High-speed ski lift that has the capacity to carry in a single chair unit all the individuals needed for a complete, self-contained mishap at the unloading point, including the skier who made the impact, the skier who got hit, the skier who ran into them, and one witness.

race A competition between two skiers to see who can get to the hospital first. See SKI PATROL.

rack lock Key-operated
security device designed to
ensure that the creep who makes
off with your skis has to spend
as much time stealing them as
you did installing that stupid rack
on the roof of your car.

rain Unwelcome form of precipitation variously referred to by ski resort personnel as liquid snow, thawed granular, dissolved powder, loose hydrous, aquapack, washed potatoes, creamed corn, or mountain dew.

recreational skier

Someone who heads to the slopes for the sheer love of skiing, not to mention the sheer love of driving long distances in heavy traffic, the sheer love of traveling with children, the sheer love of standing around and waiting in line, and the sheer love of paying enormous bills.

rental equipment

rental equipment

Boots, skis, and poles available in ski areas for a daily fee that covers normal wear and tear, regular twice-a-decade maintenance, the salaries of the personnel in work-release and witness-protection programs who work in the shops, and the original cost of obtaining the gear from landfills, recycling centers, and dumpsters.

resort Place where skiers pay an arm and a leg for the chance to break both of them. See TERRAIN.

retaining strap

Leash connecting a skier's leg to the binding so the ski remains attached during a fall, sometimes referred to as a safety strap or powder cord but more commonly known as a "zap strap," "waste lace," "croak rope," "snuff lariat," "doom lanyard," or "death thong."

rope tow

The simplest surface lift, consisting of a continuously moving rope that skiers grab onto to be pulled uphill. Rope tows can cause sore arms, but when running properly they rarely produce horrible lift lines and even when seriously malfunctioning usually don't produce horrible headlines.

run A single circuit up and down a mountain, typically involving one or more hits, a few foul tips, a beaning or two, at least one dramatic slide, a couple of close calls, and several errors.

schuss Onomatopoetic German word for a fast, straight run directly down the fall line, generally performed by a schowoff, a hotschott, a schitthead, a douschebag, or an aschhole.

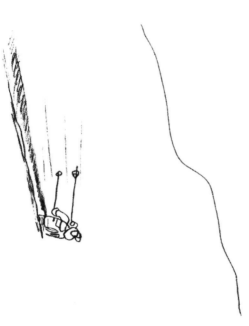

schuss

shin The bruised area on the front of the leg that runs from the point where the ache from the wrenched knee ends to the place where the soreness from the strained ankle begins.

short skis

Stable, maneuverable skis about two-thirds the length of conventional equipment that are used primarily as a teaching tool to make it possible for a beginner to progress in just a day or two from 120-centimeter skis to 150-centimeter crutches.

shovel

shovel *1.* Upwardly curved front end of a ski. *2.* Necessary tool when all that is visible following a skier's fall is the front ends of a pair of skis.

sidestepping

Method of ascending a steep slope by setting the skis into the snow in a series of short parallel steps in a motion exactly like climbing a flight of stairs sideways, often completed with a motion exactly like falling down a flight of stairs sideways.

skating

Technique in which a skier crosses flat areas by stepping from one ski to the other while pushing off from the edges, whose chief value is for the absentminded or altitude-dazed winter sports nut who arrives at an ice rink with a pair of skis or suddenly realizes that no one else in the lift line has brought a long hockey stick.

ski One of a pair of long, thin, flat, flexible runners that permit a skier to move rapidly across deep snow into deep trouble.

ski

ski boards
Very short, zippy, pole-less, easily portable, sawed-off skis that make it possible for a ski boarder to be already waiting in a lift line while traditional skiers are still back at the airport waiting in the oversize baggage claim area.

ski brake
Ingenious spring-loaded device attached to ski bindings that digs a pair of prongs into the snow to keep a ski from sliding away after a fall. Sadly, the ski industry has been slow to introduce other safety features, like the parka air bag, edible ski poles, and bar stool seat belts at après-ski watering holes.

ski bum Slang term for someone who, because he would rather ski than work, takes a low-paying job at a ski resort so he can watch people with high-paying jobs ski while he is working.

ski bunny Slang term for an attractive young female skier who hangs around upscale ski resorts in the hope that any moguls she runs into will fall head over heels for her rather than the other way around.

ski construction

Skis have undergone revolutionary refinements in recent years, but prospective purchasers should forget terms like "torsion box" and "sintered base" and focus on recognizing the two basic types of salesmen: Ultraslime (polyester clothing, artificial smile, maximum pressure, high-volume action, total heel) and Airhead (natural fiber, no rough edges, limited fact grasp, short attention span, slow uptake).

skidding Method of turning by allowing the skis to slide sideways across the snow, which is begun by flattening the skis and normally ends by flattening other skiers.

ski in, ski out

ski in, ski out

Phrase appearing in advertisements for rental lodging indicating that a nearby mountain can be directly accessed from the front door, usually with a half hour or so of cross-country skiing thrown in for free.

ski length

A simple calculation based on your height, weight, and experience will yield a ski length appropriate for you, but keep in mind when deciding whether to rent or purchase skis that your ideal ski length may change over time if you gain experience, or gain or lose weight, or, in extreme instances, lose height.

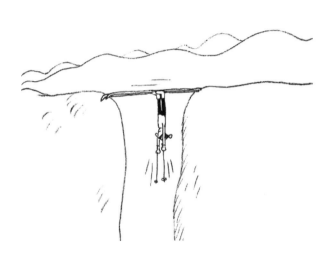

ski length

ski lift Uphill mountain transport system, either an open chairlift or an enclosed cable car, whose chief distinction is that in the chairlift you develop a cold directly from exposure to freezing winds while in the cable car you are given one by fellow skiers coughing their heads off in the cabin.

ski pants The lower portion of the outer layer of a two-piece ski suit available in a pair of popular and remarkably evenhanded styling options that offer both sexes equal mistreatment: bib pants, which make men look like hayseeds, and stretch pants, which make women look like hookers.

ski patrol A group of
trained, experienced volunteers or
professionals, wearing distinctive parkas
with white crosses, who are responsible
for maintaining safety, eliminating
dangerous conditions, and treating
injuries on the slopes. Skiers should
realize, however, that even though
members of the patrol are prepared
to respond instantly in any emergency,
a broken hot tub is not considered a
life-threatening situation, and while

patrol members do have sweeping powers, including the authority to withdraw lift privileges from reckless skiers and the sole discretion to close trails, they cannot grant divorces, order children sent to reform schools, or revoke the visas of obnoxious Europeans.

ski rack Detachable

roof-mounted device designed
to transport skis during a car
trip to the mountains, the
only run of any length during
which they are likely to remain
somewhat parallel, reasonably
well balanced, properly
pressured, and competently
steered.

ski rack

ski trip Journey taken by one or more skiers to a place where no one can remember when it snowed so little, rained so much, the spring thaw came so early, or the Chinook winds lasted so long.

slalom

Competitive event in which ski racers traverse a course marked out with gates, from the Norwegian word for "slope tracks," one of many terms Norway has given skiing, including *oops* (a fall), *blammö* (a collision with a tree), *floo* (a bad cold), *brått* (an annoyingly skillful juvenile skier), *gløpp* (food served in a ski lodge), and *dayglö* (ugly).

slope grooming

slope grooming

The process through which a slope that is unskiable because it is too deeply mogulled is transformed into one that is unskiable because it is hopelessly crowded. See SNOWCAT.

snowboarding

Radical and revolutionary form of snowsliding based on surfing and skateboarding that was initially opposed by traditional skiers but became more widely tolerated once the resort and equipment industries joined forces to harness the sport by making it duller and harder to learn and producing gear that was less comfortable and much more expensive.

snowcat

Large, tracked vehicle used to convert a ski slope into kitty litter. See SNOWMOBILE.

snowman

snowman

Politically incorrect term for a traditional winter snow sculpture that should be referred to by a more culturally sensitive gender-neutral term like person of snow, snowmanorwomannequin, Arctic-American, or thermally challenged, differently permanent seasonal icon with special refrigeration needs.

snowmobile Small, engine-powered recreational vehicle that gives millions of people who never ventured into the wilderness before an opportunity to enjoy the peace, serenity, and solitude of a day spent riding on a glorified chain saw at 40 mph through the silent, snow-covered woods.

snowmobile

snowplow

snowplow

Stopping maneuver in which the tails of the skis are pushed out into a V shape and the insides are edged that is taught to students once they have mastered the Snow Fall, the Snow Sit, the Snow Pile, and the Snow Chew.

snowplow turn

Slow, safe, easily controlled turn based on edging and wedging the skis that is taught to beginners to give them enough confidence to ski down the fall line and thus achieve the first level of skill in skiing: the ability to trip and fall over objects other than those they brought with them.

snow snake

Invisible, malevolent creature whom skiers blame for causing their falls. Other evil denizens of the slopes include the rack rat, who knocks over propped-up skis; the pole cat, who snatches poles from skiers' hands on the chairlift; and the piste weasel, who tricks them into thinking they can ski down a ridiculously difficult course.

sock

Woven foot covering made of silk, wool, or artificial fibers. The formula for determining how many pairs of which type to wear is simple: the ideal fit in a ski boot is always achieved with a combination of socks that have two-thirds the thickness of any two pairs or one-third more thickness than any one pair.

spring skiing

Treacherous environment found in March and April when due to warm weather ski trails can be covered with granular "corn" snow, icy "boilerplate," frozen "chicken heads," or slushy "mashed potatoes" and because of Easter vacation the trails are filled with partying students or "scumballs," obnoxious children or "creeps," out-of-practice once-a-year skiers or "mogul bait," and fallen beginners or "slope potatoes."

stance The correct stance

is an essential part of skiing.
Your knees should be flexed but
shaking slightly; your ankles should
be bent but wobbly; your feet
should be slightly apart and
quaking noticeably in your boots;
your arms should be straight and
covered with a good layer of
gooseflesh; your hands should

be forward, your palms clammy, your knuckles white, and your fingers crossed; your upper body should be bathed in sweat and your stomach should be knotted; your head should be up, your eyes crossed, your mouth open, and your lips quivering; and you should be mumbling audibly, "No, no, *no*" or "Why, *why*?"

stem turn

A turn in which the tail of one ski is pushed into a half-snowplow as the other ski is brought alongside, taught to skiers so they can ski across and down a slope with their skis parallel and thus achieve the second level of skill in skiing: the ability to crash into other skiers instead of waiting for other skiers to crash into them.

I   II   III   IV   V

stem turn

step turn

Technique for changing direction in which the weight is transferred from one ski to the other, taught to skiers so they can make uphill traverses, ski faster, and thus achieve the third level of skiing skill: the ability to crash into skiers above them on a slope as well as below them and to crash into more than one skier at any one time.

student Someone who

can't remember a single thing taught by a highly experienced professional who has forgotten more about skiing than most people ever learn, including a resolution never to get caught dead teaching it. See TEACHING SYSTEM.

summer skiing

It's possible to ski year-round on artificial slopes or wheeled skis, but most resorts have built golf courses, and many skiers play golf, probably because the links and the slopes have so much in common: strange equipment, stupid clothing, huge fees for daily outings, long waits, knee- and back-wrenching motions, baffling lessons, and plenty of mean-spirited competition.

T-bar A drag lift that can accommodate two skiers. A word of warning to individuals unfamiliar with this system: the T-bar starts with a jerk, and, if skiing alone, you're likely to end up riding it with a jerk.

teaching system

An incomprehensible series of explanations given to skiers for a large number of unwarranted conclusions based on inaccurate observations of irrelevant details.

teaching system

telemarking

Centuries-old Nordic skiing technique that uses modified cross-country equipment to ascend and descend steep backcountry slopes, thus making it possible for a skier to be bored stiff and scared silly all in the space of an hour.

terrain The overall physical features of a resort, which typically include some runs as steep as its prices, some as filled with bumps as its beds, some as leisurely as its service, some as slippery as its desk clerks, and some as narrow and tight as its rooms.

terrain park

Special area at a ski resort with halfpipes, mounds, and jumps sculpted by snow-shaping equipment where skiers, snowboarders, and ski bladers practice moves that are almost as hair-raising as the maneuvers they performed trying to nab a spot in a nearby parking lot.

Thor Thcandinavian god
of acheth and painth.
Thee ULLR.

tip

tip *1.* The front end of the ski, which curves upward and comes to a point. *2.* A piece of skiing advice or information, such as "Excuse me, but inasmuch as the front ends of your skis neither curve upward nor come to a point, I conclude that you have them on backwards."

toboggan Wide, flat-bottomed sled used by the ski patrol to transport injured skiers down the mountain. Its name is akin to a Micmac Indian phrase, *Toh-pah-kinn,* which translates roughly as "So long, sucker."

"track left" & "track right"

Shouts made by a skier descending a slope to let others on the trail ahead know that someone is coming down the hill. Two other warnings skiers should be aware of are "Ski!" (which warns that a loose ski is coming down the hill) and "Avalanche!" (which warns that a hill is coming down the hill).

trail
A place on a ski slope where the lift line moves a little faster. See TRAIL MAP and TRAIL RATING.

trail map

An accurately scaled, color-coded representation of the layout and location of all the trails, lifts, and other facilities of the area you are skiing, printed on a sheet of durable, foldable glossy paper that is in the pocket of an article of clothing you decided not to wear today.

trail rating

A symbolic designation of the difficulty of a slope, indicated by a green circle for the easiest, a blue square for intermediate, and one or more black diamonds for expert, which should be taken with a grain of salt since many "green" slopes have "blue" areas and a lot of "blue" slopes have "black" areas, and consequently most skiers have black and blue areas.

traverse To cross level terrain by skating or poling. Since this is a tedious process, thoughtful skiers try to come into flat areas with enough speed and momentum to give a "free lift" to a skier who "ran out of gas" or an unexpected "jump start" to someone stalled on the trail ahead with a hood up.

tree
Large form of vegetation regarded by skiers as a dangerous nuisance, despite the fact that although you may ski into a tree, one will never ski into you or try to cut in front of you in the tree line, and unless there is an avalanche, no tree will ever try to beat you down the mountain or come crashing into the room next door at two in the morning.

tree

tuning skis

tuning skis

Flattening and waxing the bases and sharpening the edges of a pair of skis to eliminate concavity (which makes them "hooky" or "grabby") or convexity (which makes them "squirrelly"). Skiers can do this themselves (which makes them "cranky," "crabby," or "grouchy"), or they can pay a bundle to have it done at a ski shop (which makes them "sulky" or "ornery").

turn Any change in the position of skis that leads to a change in direction, a change of clothes or equipment, or, in extreme cases, a change in vacation plans.

two-piece snowsuit

1. Type of ski wear with separate jacket and pants. 2. Type of personal injury litigation with two separate complaints against one skier or a pair of complaints against two separate skiers.

two-wax system

Simplified waxing procedure for Nordic skis that uses just two waxes—one for below-freezing temperatures and one for above—to produce the entire range of terrible tracking conditions it once took over a dozen different waxes to achieve.

Ullr Scandinavian deity and
pagan patron saint of skiers,
condominium salesmen,
and orthopedic surgeons.

unweighting

Quick upward or downward movement of the hips, knees, and ankles at the beginning of a turn which, if done properly, takes some of the skier's weight off the skis, making turning easier, and if done improperly takes all the skier's weight off the skis and transfers it to the hips, knees, elbows, arms, and head.

up The direction in skiing
in which nothing goes
by itself, except prices.

variable conditions

Term used to indicate that the current state of the snow surface at a given resort ranges anywhere from merely crummy to really rotten, totally awful, absolutely atrocious, or completely unskiable.

variable conditions

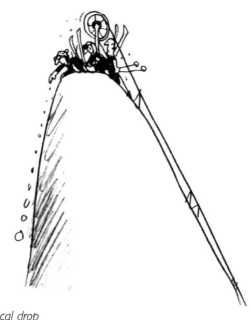

vertical drop

vertical drop

The maximum length of skiable
downhill terrain as measured
from a skier standing at the
foot of the offloading ramp
at the end of the highest lift
on the summit to the glove,
pole, hat, or wallet he or she
dropped in deep snow at the
base of the mountain.

vest Sleeveless garment that permits skiers to simultaneously have heat rashes on their torsos and chilblains on their arms. See WINDCHILL.

videotape

Important teaching
tool that helps speed
the process of turning
a novice into a menace.

waist *1.* The narrowest part of a modern shaped ski. *2.* The widest part of a traditional out-of-shape skier.

warming hut

Convivial shelter on the slopes where skiers can get together, drink hot chocolate, and swap respiratory ailments.

waterproof

Term used to describe
the ability of a garment to
repel exterior moisture for
366 or 731 days, depending
on the warranty.

waterskiing

The only form of skiing in which skiers can't end up in a place that is too steep for them, don't always wish they were wearing a lot more or a lot less clothing, never have to worry about ice, and won't ever run into a Swedish kindergarten student who is a hundred times better than they are.

waxless skis

Cross-country skis whose special patterned base ensures that they will perform unsatisfactorily even if they aren't coated with the wrong wax.

whiteout

Zero-visibility condition caused by a combination of snow and fog or low clouds in which not only can't you see the hand in front of your face, you're not even sure if it's yours.

wicking The process through which the high-tech fabric in the bottom layer of a ski outfit draws moisture away from the skin and deposits it in the crotch.

windchill

A measure of how cold it actually feels obtained by reducing the actual temperature to reflect the velocity of the wind, the relative humidity, the effects of a cold front or cold rear, the instability caused by the rapid approach of a high-pressure skiing area, and the low-level disturbance produced by a collision with a stationary mass stalled in a lift line.

yodel
Traditional Alpine call distinguished by a rapid shift from an ordinary pitch to a sharp, warbled falsetto that takes experts years to perfect but that amateurs can convincingly imitate if during a fast downhill run their skis pass on either side of a trail-marking stake.

yodel

zipper Handy fastener found on skiwear that can be easily operated by anyone who can pick his or her nose while wearing oven mitts.

About the Authors

HENRY BEARD is the author of the well-defined dictionaries *Fish•ing, Sail•ing,* and *Golf•ing,* as well as *Zen for Cats* and *The Official Exceptions to the Rules of Golf.* He is the original editor of *National Lampoon.*

ROY MCKIE illustrated all the well-defined dictionaries. He also illustrated many Dr. Seuss Beginning books, which have over 20 million copies in print.